www.tredition.de

Arsham Kasparian

Code to eternal life

The only way to the kingdom of heaven

© 2018 Arsham Kasparian
Übersetzung: Klara Böcker

Verlag und Druck: tredition GmbH, Hamburg

ISBN
Paperback: 978-3-7469-4588-0
Hardcover: 978-3-7469-4589-7
e-Book: 978-3-7469-4590-3

Arsham Kasparian

Code to eternal life

The only way to the kingdom of heaven

Contents

Chapter 5

The redemptive sacrifice of Jesus Christ as fundament of the Christian faith and the act of the New Birth

Chapter 6

The personal, oral confession as act of obedience for the New Birth

Chapter 7

What kind of gifts a person receives from God, but only through the New Birth

Chapter 8

Enough „busy work"

Chapter 9

Spiritual life of daily victory for those who are born again

<u>Code</u> of eternal life -

The only way to the kingdom of heaven

<u>Introduction</u>

First, it is my pleasant duty and joy as this book's author to explain what I meant with the title:

„Code to eternal life"

The word **"Code"** has according to Wikipedia different meanings:

Here the word **"Code"** is used as a password. And this password is one **way** to a certain **goal**.

Usually – or commonly –, a code consists of a set combination of letters and numbers. And nowadays it is very known and common for every small or big company to have their own, unique set of secret codes through which all activities, such as services, financial structures etc. are introduced or secured.

These codes overflow into all sectors of economy, private life, medicine, school as security passwords and secure access to valuable safes with secret records, documents and the way to scientific research results.

Our book title "Code to eternal life" is explained and means that God, the creator of the universe, explained in his word, the Bible, the code as key and way to get eternal life through one bible verse.

Naturally, this key (verse) is only for those who received the grace of God not only to read and to understand but to apply this biblical code (verse) or to crack it in faith.

The result of being able to crack this code is incredibly important for people, - then (when Jesus was alive) and also for people today – and until our Lord Jesus Christ, son of God **returns**.

The code for eternal life with God is:

NBJ3V3

N	=	New
B	=	Born
J	=	John
3	=	3. Chapter
V	=	Verse
3	=	3

This is the biblical word in John chapter 3, verse 3:

Jesus replied, "Very truly I tell you, no one can see the kingdom of God unless they are born again"

If someone reads God's word in John 3 verse 3 faithfully and understands the way it's meant – <u>without</u> philosophizing and raising themselves above (especially in Christian communities) to distinguish oneself as very intellectual, religious, devout personality – then God's word came to its purpose and goal.

If you read this code John 3, 3 to a child in 3rd or 4th grade, slow and stressed and then asks the child: What did you understand? I, as the author, am convinced, that the child will promptly answer: Only a Newborn person can enter heaven. Thus, millions/billions of people from all races and nations of earth will understand or interpret John 3, 3 the same as the child after they read the verse in their language – without further thinking about it. Maybe other children or adults will say it differently: Nobody can spend eternity with God if they were not born new first.

<u>Author's incidental remark:</u>

While writing and formulating the book I tried to write as easy and understandable as possible, that not only academics or scholars can read and understand the contents but everyone understands and experiences faith.

Also, I read the bible verse in German, Arabic, English and Armenic and always understood it in the same clarity as a child.

Hence results the crucial and valid question:

„If people don't go to heaven, where else do they go?"

The answer: God's word says that if one does not go to heaven and life eternally with God and his son Jesus Christ, one will end in eternal damnation and experience this with **a lot of** pain and suffering. This fact as biblical truth, if you don't go to heaven, you go into eternal damnation, results in a new question: Who is responsible for so many people dying that weren't born new and therefore won't life with God and his son Jesus Christ eternally?

This valuable question addresses the following people: The ones who teach and preach God's word (priests, pastors, bishops, evangelists and teachers etc. in different churches, Christian congregations, schools and faculties, etc.) but also the parents, grandparents, good loyal friends and the people who care for immigrants and minorities. God gave us His word through the bible and let his son Jesus Christ be crucified on Golgotha so that we can not only hear, believe and act upon His word for our worldly life but His biggest burning, holy matter close to His heart was that all people, after living a worldly life, for all people to live with Him and His son eternally. Look at chapter 6.

Gods holy will is that this part from the bible in John 3, verse 3 – our code – is our only way to the kingdom of heaven,

which will happen through Jesus:

John 14, 6 (NIV)

I am the way and the truth and the life.

No one comes to the Father except through me.

Naturally, this applies for everyone as the only way to the kingdom of heaven. And it is beautiful, awesome and very terrifying in the churches if the responsible people (pastors, priests, ministers etc.) preach this news of new birth John 3, 3 – as fast as possible – with highest priority (in first place) and the put it as goal for all activities. Nobody except for God can know when a person dies from a heart attack or an accident and was not informed enough or not with enough passion and emphasis about the Good News and therefore missed the chance to become son or daughter of God.

One can go to bed and sleep well at night only if one, as responsible and active Christian, did everything in one's power and through God's help to make sure people don't perish.

And we as confident Christians all over the world who believe that John 3, 3 is the only way to heaven, should be eager – and not let go – to make sure our loved ones, our friends and contacts will get to heaven through Newbirth. Through Newbirth, we receive the Holy Spirit, who woke Jesus Christ from the dead. That is why we are not scared of terror attacks, earthquakes or tsunamis because through rebirth we have the Holy Spirit and know 100% where we will be after death.

STRONGLY WORDED:

How does it help someone if they listen to good sermons every Sunday about peace, joy or freedom and then suddenly die and they only know very little or nothing at all about Newbirth, let alone ever practiced it (further explained in chapter 1.1). I am relatively certain that all normal, loving parents have a desire for their children or grandchildren that they will not only life together for 30-40 years but rather to meet their loved ones in eternity with no end. This wish becomes reality when we make sure, **passionately, relentlessly** and insistently, that our children and grandchildren will be born new – otherwise our love to our children – to spend eternity with them – only a **daydream**.

Important notes by the author

A)

Some words and some sentences in this book are bold to understand the meaning and content better for an easier understanding of the whole topic.

B)

It is known that God's word is very broad and deep in spiritual and mental meaning. That is why some bible verses are being used more than once in different context, - not only because their meaning fits well but also because no other verse substitutes their meaning well enough. The author marked theses passages with the short remark „this verse again".

C)

Every bible verse is marked with letters (in parenthesis). These letters show the bible translation sources that are used:

NIV   = New International Version

LEB   = Lexham English Bible

NLV   = New Life Version

Chapter 1

The Newbirth that leads to the kingdom of heaven

Me, as this book's author, state: If we don't preach John 3, 3 **in first place** in our proclamations, and not use it in our sermons as goal and core (also as goal for people to find God) then we don't preach the whole Good News (salvation and deliverance from any punishment for sins and misdeed) (chapter 7) and our sermons and instructions won't bear fruits for eternity.

There to the following explanations

1) As a matter close to his heart the author repeats the following: How does it help to pay dearly for a "sheep" at Golgotha if the ONLY listen to good sermons, for example about peace, freedom, love, the psalms and what prophets and apostles said and did etc. but rarely (or not at all) about God's act of salvation through the message Newbirth with sin confession and sin repentance to get eternal life.

2) All wonderful gifts, such as speaking in tongues, prophecies, healing, also fasting don't lead to heavenly places **alone**, but are extra beautiful gifts, that one gets through Newbirth **only**. They are precious gifts for those who are born new or **for God's sons and daughters.**

3) It is not enough if an evangelist (pastor) tells the listener to come up front, during a big event, as a brave demonstration of faith and give their heart to the lord Jesus Christ. However, it is God's gift of grace that the listener realizes that Jesus Christ is the only war to eternity. (I am the way and the truth and the life) – But this person, that walks through God's grace and power to the front made the **1st step**.

The **2nd step** is that the one who comes up front, bravely, will confess their sins and repent, full of humility and faithful belief. This will be further discussed in the next chapter.

4) It is also not enough if one was only baptized though God's grace as a baby or if one is baptized as adult through God's power. Baptism is an act of obedience that God finds joy in but it is not enough to get to heaven. If it were enough, at least 10 passages from the New Testament about converting with sin confession and repentance would have to be deleted or removed from the bible.

5) All earthly and religiously motivated actions and deeds (e.g. national or international missions trips), **to** get eternal life without rebirth are only air bubbles that will burst.

<u>Titus 3, 4-5</u> (NIV)

But when the kindness and love of God our Savior appeared, he saved us, not because of righteous things we had done, but because of his mercy. He saved us through the washing of rebirth and renewal by the Holy Spirit.

God is sovereign

The big almighty God is creator of all cosmos (sun, moon, stars, galaxies etc.) but He's also creator of every person. The entire creation is not only his work by his hands but all of creation belongs to him alone. That's why God, the almighty one, in highest, fullest freedom and sovereignty decided who of all people will get to enter his kingdom of heaven and how and under which circumstances they are allowed to.

Obviously the almighty God was and is and will always be sovereign – until the end of time. God's word talks about how in the Old and New Testament he translated some people through His sovereign decision, without them being born again.

Through God's word (and only through God's word), we read that God loved the world enough that he sacrificed his only beloved son Jesus Christ as work of salvation. Through this sacrifice of his son, he put the only concrete way to be saved in place, through his son's work of salvation. And his son confirmed this.

„I am the way, the truth and the life". This way that God declared through his son (Highway to Heaven) can only be Newborn people make use of fully. The reborn are allowed entering the kingdom of heaven only because their body is qualified. They are the only ones whose body is suitable be-cause they believe with confidence and through God's power that God's son, Jesus Christ, carried their sins as sub-stitute for them to the cross of Golgotha and as confirmation of their faith, that Jesus Christ is their redeemer, they con-fessed their sins orally and repented.

To formulate this precisely:

There is only one godly, holy way through our Lord Jesus Christ to get to heaven for us who live in New Testament time, this through our book code John 3, verse 3. I as the author want to explain this thoroughly in the next chapters.

Chapter 2

Why Newbirth is incredibly important and

crucial

In the introduction and 1st chapter we got to know that the code to eternal life (that is the way to eternity)

(this verse again)

John 3 verse 3

Is, in which Jesus Christ, son of God, tells Nicodemus:

<u>Very truly I tell you,</u>

<u>no one can see the kingdom</u>

<u>of God unless they are born again.</u>

If we believe in this godly truth, we have the full right to ask the question: why do all people, who life on our blue planet, have to be born new to get surely to the kingdom of heaven after ending their life on this world? Because our body is un-qualified by birth to enter the kingdom of heaven due to Adam's original sin.

Psalm 51, 5 (NIV)

Surely I was sinful at birth, sinful from the time my mother conceived me.

And God confirmed this in his word in

1. Corinthians 15, 50 (NIV)

I declare to you, brothers and sisters, that flesh and blood cannot inherit the kingdom of God, nor does the perishable inherit the imperishable.

Why is our body of flesh and blood by birth fading and not suitable to life in the kingdom of God for eternity? There are **two** strongly working and crucial reasons for each person, that contaminate their bodies and make them unfit for the kingdom of heaven:

The **1ˢᵗ reason** is the **original sin** from the Fall of Man by Adam and Eve, which sadly some Christians think of as fairy tale rather than biblical godly truth.

The **2nd reason** is our **own sin**, misdemeanor and misdeeds, that we did for ages and will do.

The 1st reason: Original sin

To explain original sin easily and comprehensive (also for children easy to understand) we will have to look at God's creation story in the Old Testament.

Summarized compact explanation:

In Genesis 1, 26 it says God's popular word:

Then God said, "Let us make mankind in our image, in our likeness, so that they may rule over the fish in the sea and the birds in the sky, over the livestock and all the wild animals, and over all the creatures that move along the ground."

With his son's help, God first created Adam and then took one of Adam's ribs to create Eve. Originally, God made Adam and Eve perfect and good so that their bodies were qualified to live with God and hiss on Jesus Christ millions of years joyful and happily without an end and **without Newbirth.**

And God as creator looked at his creation Adam and Eve, which he created with his son Jesus Christ and thought it was absolutely great and beautiful. And full of admiration and godly love he created a big, beautiful garden, the paradise, for his loved ones, Adam and Eve, and he filled it with a kinds of plants, created all kinds of animals that fly, walk on earth and swim in the seas and oceans. And God said to Adam and Eve: you can live here years and years to come, generous, and enjoy everything from plants and animals, except for one tree, the tree of knowledge, you can't eat from that one. But if you eat, you will be condemned and die.

God's word says in Genesis 3, 1-7 (NIV)
Now the serpent was more crafty than any of the wild animals the Lord God had made. He said to the woman, "Did God really say, 'You must not eat from any tree in the garden'?"

The woman said to the serpent, "We may eat fruit from the trees in the garden, but God did say, 'You must not eat fruit from the tree that is in the middle of the garden, and you must not touch it, or you will die.'"

"You will not certainly die," the serpent said to the woman. "For God knows that when you eat from it your eyes will be opened, and you will be like God, knowing good and evil."

When the woman saw that the fruit of the tree was good for food and pleasing to the eye, and also desirable for gaining wisdom, she took some and ate it. She also gave some to her husband, who was with her, and he ate it. Then the eyes of both of them were opened, and they realized they were naked; so they sewed fig leaves together and made coverings for themselves.

God was very sad and angry with Adam and Eve and he did not only punish them by throwing them out of paradise but Adam had to work hard and Eve has pain while childbirth and he damned their bodies with death and eternal forsakenness (damnation).

The proof in God's word:

Genesis 3, 16 -19 (NIV)

To the woman he said, "I will make your pains in childbearing very severe; with painful labor you will give birth to children. Your desire will be for your husband, and he will rule over you." To Adam he said, "Because you listened to your wife and ate fruit from the tree about which I commanded you, 'You must not eat from it,' "Cursed is the ground because of you; through painful toil you will eat food from it all the days of your life. It will produce thorns and thistles for you, and you will eat the plants of the field. By the sweat of your brow you will eat your food until you return to the ground, since from it you were taken; for dust you are and to dust you will return."

Here original sin is explained:

By Adam and Eve's procreation, all of damnation came onto their children and children's children and through all generations and all people, that life and will life on our blue planet.

Here are **only some** of many selected passages on Adam and Eve's original sin:

Romans 5, 18 (LEB)

Consequently therefore, as through one trespass came condemnation to all people, so also through one righteous deed came justification of life to all people.

Romans 5, 21 (LEB)

So that just as sin reigned in death, so also grace would reign through righteousness to eternal life through Jesus Christ our Lord.

Psalm 51,7 (NIV) (This verse again)

Surely I was sinful at birth, sinful from the time my mother conceived me.

Explanation: Here people can distinctly see the original sins awful consequence. When were still in our mother's womb, we were already sinful people even though we did not lie, did not desire, did not steal yet. Paul always suffered from the original sin.

Romans 7, 19 (NLV) Paul moans

I do not do the good I want to do. Instead, I am always doing the sinful things I do not want to do.

Romans 7, 24 (NLV) Paul moans again:

There is no happiness in me! Who can set me free from my sinful old self?

Romans 5, 17 (NLV)

The power of death was over all men because of the sin of one man, Adam. But many people will receive His loving-favor and the gift of being made right with God. They will have power in life by Jesus Christ.

This incredibly bad influence of original sin on our humanly bodies is so strong that we are always candidates for eternal forsakenness (damnation) and we cannot do anything about it.

We personally are helpless and powerless against the original sin. We need to understand and accept this as biblical truth:

You sin because you are a sinner right from the start – and you are not a sinner because you sin.

The core of the Christian faith is that our **lord Jesus Christ, son of God, is the only one** of all people, religions and sects who achieved victory through his sacrifice at Golgotha over the **original sin** and dark powers and our, through original sin damned body was **nailed** to the **cross** at Golgotha.

Which means every reborn person is free of all damnation by original sin.

Romans 6, 6 (NIV)

For we know that our old self was crucified with him so that the body ruled by sin might be done away with,[a] that we should no longer be slaves to sin

The **2nd reason**

The second strongly acting crucial reason why the human body is contaminated for the kingdom of heaven and unfit, **is our own sin**.

Romans 3, 23 u. 24 (NIV)

For all have sinned and fall short of the glory of God, and all are justified freely by his grace through the redemption that came by Christ Jesus.

Chapter 3

Contractions (as urgent necessity) – condition for Newbirth

It is widely known that an expecting mother will experience incredibly painful contractions near the end of pregnancy (I was with my wife when she had our 3 children). I assume the following (this is an assumption and not written in God's word) that God thought that (our Code John 3, 3 "born again") humans have to experience such strong spiritual contractions and a strong passionate wish before he can be born again by the Holy Spirit.

Otherwise the godly holy **act of rebirth** would be a superficial, spontaneous (without personal want for necessary spiritual change) experiment, by which one would never know if it works or not.

Some contractions for spiritual rebirth (e.g.)

1) If one suffers strongly from no fulfilment in their spiritual existence and a strong need for personal and spiritual change – then a person is fit for spiritual rebirth.

2) If one has a strong desire to be freed from their strong depression, their sadness and strong mental drain – then a person is fit for spiritual rebirth.

3) If one has a strong desire for mental and spiritual change because of their **bad conscience** (by burden through transgression and sins, that one did for years) and is scared of eternal damnation after God's word in

Ephesians 2, 1 (NIV)

As for you, you were dead in your transgressions and sins

- Then the person is very well fit for spiritual Newbirth.

4) If one has a string desire for spiritual or mental change even though everything worldly and materialistically (wealth, house, job, health, money etc.) one wished for, pursued and

achieved, but still no fulfilment of meaning and no joy in life – then the person is fit for personal Newbirth.

5) With strong contractions – **without Newbirth** – we life our whole lives without godly leading through the Holy Spirit, which only reborn, God's sons and daughters, will get, according to Galatians 4, verse 6.

<u>**Galatians 4, 6**</u> (NIV)

Because you are his sons, God sent the Spirit of his Son into our hearts, the Spirit who calls out, "Abba, Father."

Chapter 4

Why faith in Jesus Christ's sacrifice is the irreplaceable way to heaven

God's word in **1. Corinthians 15, 50** says

That our body is contaminated through the original sin and unfit for the kingdom of heaven and only through faith in Jesus Christ's sacrifice on the cross and our conversion will our body a new creation as written in 2. Corinthians 5, 17 and this new body is fit for the kingdom of heaven.

Before we will hear in chapter 5 in which way our lord Jesus Christ gave his body as redemption for all people, who believe in his sacrifice, we want to explore in chapter 4, why God didn't use another human like a prophet, apostle, priest etc. for the act of salvation but chose only Jesus Christ,

A) Because Jesus Christ, son of God, was originally created by God

And didn't descent from Adam and Eve, - his body if free of any kind of damnation by Adam and Eve.

The following **7 selected** passages from God's word testify that **Jesus was created by God**.

Jesus talks to his heavenly father:

1)

Hebrews 10, 5 (HB)

Therefore, when Christ came into the world, he said: "Sacrifice and offering you did not desire, but a body you prepared for me; with burnt offerings and sin offerings you were not pleased. Then I said, 'Here I am — it is written about me in the scroll — I have come to do your will, my God.'

Explanation:

Before Jesus was born by Mary, he was with God, his father in a spiritual state.

2)

To further emphasize this (this verse again):

John 3, 16 + 17 (NLV)

For God so loved the world that He gave His only Son. Who-ever puts his trust in God's Son will not be lost but will have life that lasts forever. For God did not send His Son into the world to say it is guilty. He sent His Son so the world might be saved from the punishment of sin by Him.

Explanation:

The word „to give" means that someone owns something and wants to give it away. The word "to send" means also that Jesus was with God in heaven and was sent to earth as human by being given a human body so that Jesus could live as human under humans and fulfil his act of salvation.

3)

Ephesians 1, 3-5 + 7 (NIV)

Let us honor and thank the God and Father of our Lord Jesus Christ. He has already given us a taste of what heaven is like. Even before the world was made, God chose us for Himself because of His love. He planned that we should be holy and without blame as He sees us. God already planned to have us as His own children. This was done by Jesus Christ. In His plan God wanted this done. Because of the blood of Christ, we are bought and made free from the punishment of sin. **And because of His blood, our sins are forgiven.** His loving-favor to us is so rich.

Explanation:

Jesus was with God in a spiritual state before the universe existed.

Romans 8, 29 (NIV)

For those God foreknew he also predestined to be conformed to the image of his Son, that he might be the firstborn among many brothers and sisters.

Explanation:

Jesus Christ was created, as first born, before Mary, Jesus's mother was.

4)

I, as the author, am convinced that the trinity existed before Jesus was born to Mary.

5)

Hebrews 5, 5 (NLV)

It is the same way with Christ. He did not choose the honor of being a Religious Leader Who has made the way for man to go to God. Instead, God said to Christ, "You are My Son. Today I have become Your Father."

6)

Psalm 2,7 (NLV)

I will make known the words of the Lord. He said to Me, "You are My Son. Today I have become Your Father."

7)

Genesis 1, 26 (this verse again) (NIV)

Then God said, "Let us make mankind in our image, in our likeness, so that they may rule over the fish in the sea and the birds in the sky, over the livestock and all the wild animals, and over all the creatures that move along the ground."

Explanation:

Jesus Christ, God's son, helped his heavenly father while creating humans and created Mary's ancestors.

B) Because Jesus Christ is the only person who never sinned in his

…because God can't sin

1)

Hebrews 4, 15 (NLV)

Our **Religious Leader** understands how weak we are. Christ was tempted in every way we are tempted, but He did **not sin**.

2)

2. Corinthians 5, 21 (NIV)

God made him who had no sin to be sin for us, so that in him we might become the righteousness of God.

3)

1. Peter 2, 22 + 24 (NIV)

He committed no sin, and no deceit was found in his mouth. He himself bore our sins in his body on the cross, so that we might die to sins and live for righteousness;

4)

Colossians 2, 9 (NIV)

For in Christ all the fullness of the Deity lives in bodily form,

Comment: the son of God does not sin

C) Because – only through Jesus Christ, God wanted to have his son's brothers and sisters

The reborn people will not only come to the kingdom of heaven as fully entitled citizens but also as sons and daughters of God, who will life in the same house as their heavenly father.

1)

Once again, the following verse as a proof that Jesus was with God before the universe was created:

Ephesians 1, 3-5+7   (HB)

Let us honor and thank the God and Father of our Lord Jesus Christ. He has already given us a taste of what heaven is like. Even before the world was made, God chose us for Himself because of His love. He planned that we should be holy and without blame as He sees us. **God already planned to have us as His own children.** This was done by Jesus Christ. In His plan God wanted this done. Because of the blood of Christ, we are bought and made free from the punishment of sin. And because of His blood, our sins are forgiven. His loving-favor to us is so rich.

And God confirmed in the following text that the Newborns, who believe in Jesus sacrifice and act of salvation, are chosen from the beginning of time to become brothers and sisters of Jesus Christ.

2)

<u>Romans 8, 29</u> (NLV) (this verse again)

For those God foreknew he also predestined to be con-formed to the image of his Son, that <u>he might be the firstborn among many brothers and sisters</u>.

If one accepts the 2 previous verses deeply through faith and accepts them as a godly unshaken truth, that Jesus Christ, don of god, is our heavenly brother then it refreshes our soul as fresh air for our faith in God's word.

3)

<u>Galatians 4, 6-7</u> (NIV)

Because you are his sons, God sent the Spirit of his Son into our hearts, the Spirit who calls out, "Abba, Father." So you are no longer a slave, but God's <u>child</u>; and since you are <u>his child</u>, God has made you also an heir.

4)

<u>2. Corinthians 6, 18</u> (NIV)

And, "I will be a Father to you, and you will be my sons and daughters, says the Lord Almighty."

D) Because God loved the people so much that HE gave his only son a **living bodyguard** for every reborn person.

<u>**Matt. 28,20**</u> (NLV)

And teaching them to obey everything I have commanded you. And surely I am with you always, to the very end of the age.

Chapter 5

Jesus Christ's sacrifice as foundation of the Christian faith and the act of rebirth

In this book's chapter 2 and 3 God's word was explained by using the bible verse

Ephesians 2, 1 (NIV) (this verse again)

As for you, you were dead in your transgressions and sins

Therefore, God the creator of this universe looked at his creation and saw that many people are spiritually dead because of the original sin and also their own sinful way of life. This happened on the day when Adam and Eve were banned from paradise and damned due to the fall. God was very strict with people who sinned in the Old Testament's time. This concerned especially parents.

Exodus 34, 7 (NIV)

(…) Yet he does not leave the guilty unpunished; he punishes the children and their children for the sin of the parents to the third and fourth generation.

And God saw all people through all times as dead who are not qualified for the kingdom of heaven due to the original sin and their own sins. No human works and achievements to please the righteous God and get to heaven were enough. In addition, all animal sacrifices in the Old Testament, e.g. burnt offerings, sin offerings could not redeem or replace any **punishments for sin**.

Hebrews 10, 1-2 (NLV)

The Law is like a picture of the good things to come. The Jewish religious leaders gave gifts on the altar in worship to God all the time year after year. Those gifts could not make the people who came to worship perfect. If those gifts given to God could take away sins, the people who came to worship would no longer feel guilty of sin. They would have given no more gifts.

And exactly that is what our Lord Jesus Christ, God's son, did for us with his one sacrifice by giving his godly body on the cross of Golgotha as punishment for all sin and misdeeds of humanity so that they will be freed from any kind of damnation and have a **good conscience**.

Hebrews 10, 3-6 (NLV)

When they gave the gifts year after year, it made them remember that they still had their sins. The blood of animals cannot take away the sins of men. When Christ came to the world, He said to God, "You do not want animals killed or gifts given in worship. You have made My body ready to give as a gift. You are not pleased with animals that have been killed or burned and given as gifts on the altar to take away sin.

Hebrews 10, 7-9 (NLV)

Then I said, 'I have come to do what You want, O God. It is written in the Law that I would.' Then Christ said, "You do not want animals killed or gifts given in worship to you for sin. You are not pleased with them." These things are done because the Law says they should be done. Then He said, "I have come to do what You want Me to do." And this is what He did when He died on a cross. God did away with the Old Way of Worship and made a New Way of Worship.

And God saw that all people and their religious deeds and achievements could not be righteous in the eye of God. But it was God, our great creator, who, with his godly, holy love with no end, has always sent new men and women as prophets and later apostles to warn people form eternal death or damnation and also to comfort, to heal, to be righteous in God's eyes so that one can life forever, joyful.

But none of those prophets and apostles could remove any of the human punishment for sins. Not even thousands of liters of animal blood could pay for the human punishment for sins.

Mark 12, 6

He had a much-loved son to send yet. So last of all he sent him to them, saying, 'They will respect my son.' (Much-loved son = Jesus Christ)

This was done by God who loves humanity so much that he gave his only, dearly loved son (the son who planned and helped with creation) to the world so he could save humanity from their own damnation and let them enter the kingdom of heaven.

(this verse again)

John 3, 16-17 (NLV)

For God so loved the world that He gave His only Son. Whoever puts his trust in God's Son will not be lost but will have life that lasts forever. For God did not send His Son into the world to say it is guilty. He sent His Son so the world might be saved from the punishment of sin by Him.

Our God didn't send Jesus Christ like the other prophets to preach, to warn, to comfort, to perform miracles, to heal, to prophesize but to nail his favorite one to the cross of Golgotha with lots of scorn and mockery and died in strong pain and suffering to remove all guilt and sin of humanity, so that many people can be free from all damnation and born new and will enter the kingdom of heaven as HIS sons and daughters. It was truly His godly love to us humans that we can be saved, without any additional works and achievements, only through grace and pure convinced faith, nowadays.

More precise:

Nowadays we are allowed to believe and accept that Jesus Christ bore the **punishment** for all our sin, that we ourselves deserved, on his body so painfully that we are qualified for the kingdom of heaven.

The act of salvation

And we realized that Jesus Christ was the only one of all prophets and apostles (who were sinners) to be chosen and allowed to be ridiculed and spit on by the Jews but they also carried him as prisoner to the judge Pilate, because they (the Jews) wanted to slay and kill Jesus. Jesus had said that he was king of the Jews. Pilate did not find any guilt on Jesus Christ and wanted to set him free. But Pilate set Barnabas (a big criminal) free as the Jews (Pharisees) protested and yelled a lot and let Jesus be whipped and like a criminal they put a crown of thorns on his head and dressed him in a king's gown. And Jesus carried, with Simon from Cyrene's help, his cross to a place called Golgotha. And when they put big nails through his hands and feet, Jesus said "I am thirsty". So they gave him wine mixed with bile and after he drank this, he screamed aloud **"It is done"**. With this scream "it is done",

Jesus Christ accomplished his heavenly father's task to take all punishment for all humanity's sins onto his body and carried it with incredible pain.

The proof that the sacrifice redeemed all of humanity's sins completely was that ho rose again from the dead after 3 days and his body was completely without sin so Jesus was allowed with all godly right to sit on the right side of his heavenly father.

Hebrews 1, 3 (NLV)

The Son shines with the shining-greatness of the Father. The Son is as God is in every way. It is the Son Who holds up the whole world by the power of His Word. The Son gave His own life so we could be clean from all sin. After He had done that, He sat down on the right side of God in heaven.

And it is a big reason for Newborn people to begin and end **every day with joy** to honor Jesus Christ's big sacrifice.

Transaction (Exchange)

And God watched this exchange, the **transaction** that Jesus Christ, the righteous one, who didn't know sin and didn't sin, carried the punishment of all sins, transgressions and misdeeds of humanity with his own body in pain.

And God took his son's righteousness and gave it to everyone who believes that Jesus Christ paid the punishment, that they deserved themselves, for them.

That means: When Jesus Christ was nailed to the cross of Golgotha, Jesus was a person loaded with many big sins – just like a criminal – until his big cry of victory: "it is done". HE paid for all punishments for the original sin and the other sins **completely** and forever with this cry, "it is finished!" "It is done".

Hebrews 10, 13 – 14 (NLV)

He is waiting there for God to make of those who have hated Him a place to rest His feet. And by one gift He has made perfect forever all those who are being set apart for God-like living.

God himself confirmed this once again in his word that HE would **never punish** the punishment for sins, transgressions and misdeeds **ever again**.

Hebrews 10, 17 + 18 (NIV) (this verse again)

"Their sins and lawless acts I will remember no more." And where these have been forgiven, sacrifice for sin is no longer necessary.

That's why Jesus said: My yoke is light (only pure faith), because today every one of the 7.5 billion people living on our blue planet can live and be reborn righteously in front of God's eyes if they truly believe and testify:

a) Jesus Christ is God's son. He is my personal Redeemer, Savior and Rescuer, because he removed all punishment for my sin at the cross of Golgotha.

b) Confirmation of point a)

By **orally converting** (through confession of sin and regretting of sin)

look at the next chapter 6

Chapter 6

The personal, oral confession as act of obedience for rebirth

In this chapter, we reach the main reason and main thought and goal of this book:

The way to the kingdom of heaven and how to be reborn according to God's word.

For our creator, our big God, it is absolutely not enough, that people everywhere only hear, read and believe that Jesus Christ freed us from all our sin with his sacrifice on the cross of Golgotha.

1. Peter 2, 24 (NLV)

He carried our sins in His own body when He died on a cross. In doing this, we may be dead to sin and alive to all that is right and good. His wounds have healed you!

But, it was God's holy will that every habitant of our blue plant would confidently, **orally** confess the following:

1) That they are a sinful person and deserves eternal damnation for their sin

2) That they were freed from all damnation by the work of redemption that Jesus Christ, son of God did on the cross of Golgotha.

3) That they **orally** confess and regret every single sin they did and remember.

Those three godly orders „confess and regret sin" is called **"conversion"**.

As proof that this conversion (sin confession and sin repentance) is the way to the kingdom of heaven, I as the author, collected many bible verses from many parts of the bible:

1. John 1, 9 (NIV)

If we confess our sins, **he is faithful and just and will forgive us our sins and purify us from all unrighteousness**.

Ephesians 1,7 (NIV)

In him we have redemption through his blood, the forgiveness of sins, in accordance with the riches of God's grace

Romans 6, 6 (NIV) (this verse again)

For we know that our old self was crucified with him so that the body ruled by sin might be done away with, that we should no longer be slaves to sin

Explanation:

This is the new state of body for newborn people, that the body that was damned by Adam through original sin and was nailed to the cross of Golgotha with Jesus through conversion.

Acts 3, 19 (NIV)

Repent, then, and turn to God, so that your sins may be wiped out, that times of refreshing may come from the Lord.

Luke 24, 47 (NIV)

And repentance for the forgiveness of sins will be preached in his name to all nations, beginning at Jerusalem.

Romans 10, 10 (NIV)

For it is with your heart that you believe and are justified, and it is with your mouth that you profess your faith and are saved.

Explanation:

The previous verse states God's word clearly, that it is not enough for everyone just to read, hear and **believe** that Jesus Christ freed us from damnation with act of salvation and therefore are seen as righteous in the eye of God but it is God's holy will for us to confess and regret sin orally. Only by doing this, we are qualified for the kingdom of heaven.

Luke 15, 7 (NIV)

I tell you that in the same way there will be more rejoicing in heaven over one sinner who <u>repents</u> than over ninety-nine righteous persons who do not need to repent.

Acts 17, 30 (NIV)

In the past God overlooked such ignorance, but now he commands all people everywhere to repent.

Matthew 4, 17 (NIV)

From that time on Jesus began to preach, "Repent, for the kingdom of heaven has come near."

Luke 15, 10 (NIV)

In the same way, I tell you, there is rejoicing in the presence of the angels of God over one sinner who repents."

Mark 1, 15 (NIV)

"The time has come," he said. "The kingdom of God has come near. Repent and believe the good news!"

Naturally – as mentioned in chapter 1, God is almighty and **sovereign**. Through his grace, he can translate single people without conversion and New Birth as an exception (like in the Old Testament). It is irresponsible and not God's holy will that people generalize the word **"grace"** as if it alone was enough as the way to the kingdom of heaven without New Birth (sin confession/sin repentance). Otherwise, one can with conviction and reference of God's word claim and say:

Without conversion/New Birth – no entrance to the kingdom of heaven.

Conversion

It is God's holy will that people strive after the act of conversion with joy and cheers for the following reasons:

Only through conversion:

1. The person is a new creature (newborn body) and very fit and qualified for life in the kingdom of heaven.

2. One receives a life without bad conscience.

3. One is freed from eternal damnation (Romans 8, 1-2).

4. One receives the Spirit of the Great Awakening from Jesus Christ.

5. One's name is written in the book of life.

6. One becomes brother or sister of Jesus Christ.

7. God is not only creator but also the personal father

Comment:

These are the wonderful great **fruits of conversion** if one believes with conviction that Jesus Christ, son of God, paid for the punishment that we deserved for our sins and misdeeds on the cross of Golgotha. We can only show thankfulness to God and appreciate his son's sacrifice by living free and joyfully.

Jesus says in

John 14, 6 (NIV)

I am the way and the truth and the life. No one comes to the Father except through me.

(Conversion is the way to the kingdom of heaven)

The way to heaven was made through Jesus Christ by conversion. It is obvious that every convinced Christian can shape the act of conversion how they are lead by the spirit of God (Holy Spirit).

But sin confession and repentance have to be content of every conversion.

Practical conversion in 2 steps

Only an example:

The following 2 steps for conversion, were practiced by the author of this book himself and since approx. 50 years also used by friends, relatives or different listeners. This lead to many visible fruits.

1st step

Ask God for power to experience the New Birth

Dear God, wonderful creator, your word says in 1. Corinthians 2, 5 (so that your faith might not rest on human wisdom, but on God's power).

That is why I ask you, dear God, with all my heart that you are with me and your good, Holy Spirit will give me **power, compassion and love** so I can experience the real conversion for the kingdom of heaven and will be born new according to your word in John 3, 3.

2nd step

Prayer to the lord Jesus Christ

Jesus Chris, son of God, I thank you wholeheartedly that you thought of me when you sacrificed your **godly, holy body** 2000 years ago compensatory (representatively) **under enormous pain and suffering** for the sins and misdeeds that I deserve. And today I bow before you in full humility and obedience and confess extensive – **as far as I can remember** – my sins, misdeeds and transgressions that I did for years. (e.g. 2007 I betrayed, 2009 I lied, 2014 I gave a wrong testimony etc.)

I am wholeheartedly sorry and I regret every single sin, I did. And I thank you that you accept my repentance. Praise be to Jesus name in eternity.

A recommended order for conversion:

1. A quiet room

2. on your knees – Jesus as model

Only an example:

When I (author) converted at the age of 27, I did the following:

a) All my sins and transgressions were written down by my-self in an 18-pages long notebook.

b) I was strongly convinced that the Lord Jesus Christ paid for all my transgressions and sins that I wrote down in the 18-pages long notebook through his sacrifice on the cross of Golgotha.

c) I closed my bedroom door and put my bible on the bed and kneeled in front of it and fulfilled both conversion steps with God's help. God's answer to anyone who experienced the conversion whole-heartedly:

<u>John 8, 36</u> (NIV)

So if the Son sets you free, you will be free indeed.

Through Jesus Christ's work of salvation at Golgotha you are 100% free of any godly punishment for any sin you ever did in your life.

You cannot even get punished for those sins.

Very important to know:

Through faith in the work of salvation of Jesus Christ, we know that Jesus redeemed all sins that we deserved on the cross of Golgotha. Those who can believe this truth cannot get a bad conscience and sleep well with godly peace.

This is explainable as follows:

God's word says that our creator, or holy God, is holy, holy, holy and righteous.

I, as the author, am convinced that this holy God cannot punish anyone for his or her sins that Jesus Christ redeemed on the cross of Golgotha, because then HE would be unjust.

Further Explanation: If a defendant gets for example a 6 years long prison sentence then no other judge can prosecute the person for the same offence again.

Chapter 7

What kind of gifts a person receives from God, but only through the New Birth

The following are God's good presents that one gets right after the New Birth through **conversion;** and not prior, because that would be self-delusion.

A) New Creation – newly born

I am a new creation through Jesus Christ's sacrifice as a Newborn, who is qualified for the kingdom of Heaven.

2. Corinthians 5, 17 (NIV) (this verse again)

Therefore, if anyone is in Christ, the new creation has come: The old has gone, the new is here!

Explanation:

The old creation was **contaminated through the original sin and their own sins**. This new creation that is qualified for the kingdom of heaven is what the New Born gets by conversion (sin confession and sin repentance). This also means: The Newborns (are additionally to their human birth) born again but not from perishable semen, but through God's word (imperishable semen). It was exactly the same for Jesus Christ. He was created by his heavenly father and then born again by Mary but not from Josef's, her husband, imperishable semen.

1. Peter 1, 23 (NIV)

For you have been born again, not of perishable seed, but of imperishable, through the living and enduring word of God.

B) No damnation

The Newborn can also with reason say and claim: My heavenly father loved me personally strongly and bestowed grace by giving me his godly powers and letting me believe that his son Jesus Christ paid the punishment for my sins, misdeeds and transgressions entirely with his death on the cross and freed me from eternal damnation.

Romans 8, 1-2 (NLV)

Now, because of this, those who belong to Christ will not suffer the punishment of sin. 2 The power of the Holy Spirit has made me free from the power of sin and death. This power is mine because I belong to Christ Jesus.

C) Eternal Life

Eternal life, where there is no suffering, sickness, fear, worries but the opposite: happiness, joy, peace etc. The Newborn can with reason say and claim: I am Newborn according to God's word in John 3 verse 3 and I will have eternal life in heaven with God and hiss on Jesus Christ with no end.

(this verse again)

John 3 verse 3 according to our code

Jesus replied, "Very truly I tell you, no one can see the kingdom of God unless they are born again"

But when a person is born new, they can not only see the kingdom of heaven but also live endlessly with God and his son.

D) Having Jesus' spirit of awakening

And when I as Newborn die, the spirit that I got through New Birth, is the same as the spirit that woke Jesus from the dead – the same one will awake me from the state of death and make me come alive for the kingdom of heaven.

Romans 8, 11 (NLV)

The Holy Spirit raised Jesus from the dead. If the same Holy Spirit lives in you, He will give life to your bodies in the same way.

E) my name is written in the book of life

My name is written in the book of life as citizen of heaven and I live in God's house.

Ephesians 2, 19 (NIV)

Consequently, you are no longer foreigners and strangers, but fellow citizens with God's people and also members of his household

An easy explanation as well:

Asylum seekers and refugees took big efforts with many exertions, trouble, deprivation and expenses on themselves in order to cross the border to Germany or any other European country.

Those refugees firstly are strangers and foreigners to the German authorities and can only enter the country if they own the necessary paper work to show that they don't originate from a save country (according to the current situation). Only if they meet these requirements they are allowed to enter the country. The same way the people who are not New Born are not qualified to enter the kingdom of God.

Back to the refugees:

Only after a successful asylum procedure and later a citizenship process, which can often take years, the foreigner will be accepted as a full citizen into the community of Germans. The heavenly Newborns are completely qualified by conversion to be accepted as full citizen into the community of saints.

F) God's sons and daughters

The Newborns will not only enter the kingdom of heaven as fully entitled citizens but also as God's sons and daughters who live in the same house as their heavenly father and their brother Jesus Christ.

The Newborns are with godly reason God's sons and daughters and therefore the Lord Jesus Christ's siblings. Because Newborns believe that Jesus Christ, son of God, freed us from any punishment for our sins and transgressions with his sacrifice on the cross of Golgotha, God **automatically chooses** them as his sons and daughters and therefore **naturally** as brothers and sisters of Jesus Christ, the Lord.

Ephesians 1, 3-5+7 (NIV) (this verse again)

Let us honor and thank the God and Father of our Lord Jesus Christ. He has already given us a taste of what heaven is like. Even before the world was made, God chose us for Himself because of His love. He planned that we should be holy and without blame as He sees us. God already planned to have us as His own children. This was done by Jesus Christ. In His plan God wanted this done. Because of the blood of Christ, we are bought and made free from the punishment of sin. And because of His blood, our sins are forgiven. His loving favor to us is so rich.

And God confirmed in the following text that the Newborns, who believe in Jesus sacrifice and act of salvation, are chosen from the beginning of time to become brothers and sisters of Jesus Christ.

Romans 8, 29 (NLV) (this verse again)

For those God foreknew he also predestined to be conformed to the image of his Son, that he might be the firstborn among many brothers and sisters.

If one accepts this as a godly and unshakeable truth that Jesus Christ, God's son, is our heavenly father then this refreshes our soul as fresh air for our faith in God's word.

G) God as our heavenly father

And God himself confirmed in the next 2 bible passages that the Newborns are not only his creation but also his sons and daughters and the Newborns are allowed to call HIM "Abba" (father).

Galatians 4, 6-7 (NIV) (this verse again)

Because you are his sons, God sent the Spirit of his Son into our hearts, the Spirit who calls out, "Abba, Father." So you are no longer a slave, but God's child; and since you are his child, God has made you also an heir.

2. Corinthians 6, 18 (NIV)

I will be a Father to you, and you will be my sons and daughters, says the Lord Almighty.

This is another confirmation that we, the Newborns, are His sons and daughters and God himself is our heavenly father.

H) The Newborns have the Holy Spirit

Only Newborns as sons and daughters of God will get the Holy Spirit (the same that Jesus also has).

Once again the 2 verses as confirmation that we have the same Holy Spirit as Jesus Christ, God's son, when we are new born:

Romans 8, 11 (NLV)

This time as confirmation that we have the Holy Spirit, just like Jesus Christ.

The Holy Spirit raised Jesus from the dead. If the same Holy Spirit lives in you, He will give life to your bodies in the same way.

Galatians 4, 6 (NIV)

Because you are his sons, God sent the Spirit of his Son into our hearts, the Spirit who calls out, "Abba, Father."

I) Jesus carried our sicknesses

The newborn, convinced Christians experience a lot of consolation and help in sickness, as they believe not only that the Lord freed them from damnation and hell but also that he carried their sickness in great pain on his body.

Matthew 8, 17 (NLV)

It happened as the early preacher Isaiah said it would happen. He said, "He took on Himself our sickness and carried away our diseases."

This last verse is a great, daily consolation for suffering, groaning convinced Christians (Newborns).

J) The Newborns have a reserved heavenly apartment

Rightly, a Newborn is convinced that they get a big living space in the kingdom of heaven after their death, a luxurious apartment with all kinds of conveniences, where they do not have to pay rent or repair anything, and can live from eternity to eternity with no end.

John 14, 2 + 3 (NLV)

There are many rooms in My Father's house. If it were not so, I would have told you. I am going away to make a place for you. After I go and make a place for you, I will come back and take you with Me. Then you may be where I am.

Ephesians 2, 19-21 (NIV) (this verse again) **(look at Chap. 6 Paragraph 2),**

but this time so that we will live in God's heavenly house, after our death.

Consequently, you are no longer foreigners and strangers, but fellow citizens with God's people and also members of his household, built on the foundation of the apostles and prophets, with Christ Jesus himself as the chief cornerstone.

Chapter 8

Enough „busy work"

Our holy God and creator loved us humans (his creation) dearly and strongly so that he sent his only son to the world – and he let the Jews spit on him, laugh at him, talk bad about him and in the end crucify him with big nails with incredible suffering and strong pain.

Newborn pastors, evangelists etc. who received God's spirit (the Holy Spirit) are chosen and **worthy** to teach and preach the **whole** and **complete**

Good News about the work of salvation by Jesus Christ

and not only the part of the Good News (look at part A) so that many people will be born new and go to the kingdom of heaven live eternally with our great creator and his son Jesus Christ.

The complete Christian Good News consists of 2 parts A and B

Part A

This half of the Good News is part A, that the believers believe in Jesus Christ's work of salvation at Golgotha (look at chapter 3), that they accept Jesus Christ as good shepherd, brother, comforter, teacher and friend to live happy, successful, healthy, peaceful, but only **limited, earthly years** with this. God did absolutely **not only** let his son suffer on the cross of Golgotha in disgrace and mockery,

but God sacrificed his son also for the other half of the Good News (part B).

Part B

The big matter close to God's heart was and is, that the beautiful and intelligent creation he created with the help of his son, Jesus Christ, will not only live a happy, worldly life and afterwards be damned for eternity, but his, unimaginable, godly, holy love was that the creation (humans), who are Newborn through conversion (sin confession and sin repentance), will die as God's sons and daughters and come to him (to their creator) to reign, with him and his son, over the galaxy and live eternally with God on the huge **apartment complex**, where our heavenly father, our great creator, lives **(Ephesians 2, 19).**

More precisely:

It is absolutely not enough in God's eyes that many of the religious, Christian people in charge focus mainly on part A (= half of the Good News).

It is God's will that all through his grace assembled Christian leaders and preachers will proclaim the whole Good News which is part a and B. Sadly, in some churches and congregations only part A and very little of part B is proclaimed, rather than the whole Good News, part A and B.

This is what it looks like in daily life:

Weekly or annual work program for usual religious activities in some congregations:

Once again, the author wants to emphasize the incredible importance of the message of Newbirth id for everyone. Without continuous preaching, praying, singing about the Newbirth as God's main order (God mainly sacrificed his son for this) it results in losses of number of people that come to the kingdom of heaven. It is sadly common that the pastor, preacher etc. holds, Sunday for Sunday, only a **good** organized service about current topics and explains his preaching well and perfect. Additionally, there will be small groups and worship once a week maybe and 2 or 3 mission trips to the city center, seminars etc. This will please our heavenly father and make him happy. But maybe this hardworking pastor will only preach about **New Birth, original sin, conversion** (sin confession and sin repentance) and also about the topic "**God's sons and daughters**" once or even not at all in the whole year.

Who is responsible if one of our dear church members has an accident, dies, and is not New Born **because** they never heard about the Newbirth and conversion enough, passionately and insistently?

Who is responsible if they do not come into the kingdom of heaven with God, or creator?

As **absolute worthy congregation** qualifies one where the shepherd (pastor) looks at his "sheep" **once a week** from his pulpit and takes **inventory** on who is Newborn, who has trouble getting there and even who is completely against it.

Then God, through his spirit, will not only give the pastor power and wisdom for the right conversations with people who are interested in Newbirth but also the right prayers for these people.

Then every Sunday there will be a fragrance rising from the church's chimney into heaven and God will nourish many fruits, visible and invisible, for eternity. And those spiritually responsible for the congregation will go to bed with good and best conscience because they preached the whole gospel, the Good News.

Just as God wants, without what ifs and buts and without self-made devout theories, traditions and laws.

Visible joy about the whole Good News

The almighty God has big, godly joy in congregations, churches etc. where New Birth after John 3, 3 through conversion with sin confession and repentance is set as main goal. And this for all their Christian, religious activities like preaching, praying, singing, evangelizing etc.

Without New Birth as goal, it is impossible for people to enter the kingdom of heaven and live endlessly with God and his son. And then all activities and works of faith are only **busy work** – namely that people in Christian communities and churches only feel free, happy and well and live until death comes – then what?! What if people don't get to the kingdom of heaven because they are not qualified (because they were not born new)?

I, as author, politely want to strain the readers' imaginative power for a good purpose and show this vision towards the end of this chapter:

This would be really good:

That in many congregations and churches Sunday for Sunday son many people as **God's sons and daughters** (siblings of our Lord and savior Jesus Christ) that are through

New Birth /conversion **<u>pardoned</u>** by God and chosen to once enter the kingdom of heaven. Then the crowd of angles will start singing „hallelujah, hallelujah, hallelujah" with trombones and sing and praise and applaud about the **visible, worthy** victory of Jesus Christ over dark forces on the cross of Golgotha. These siblings from our Lord Jesus Christ are best qualified for a big **awakening**.

Chapter 9

Spiritual life of daily victory for those who are born again

The almighty God gave full, godly peace to the Newborns, because they did the **highest and holiest** what God asked of the people by fulfilling conversion (sin confession/sin repentance) obediently and with firm belief.

Romans 5, 1-2 (NLV)

Now that we have been made right with God by putting our trust in Him, we have peace with Him. It is because of what our Lord Jesus Christ did for us. 2 By putting our trust in God, He has given us His loving-favor and has received us. We are happy for the hope we have of sharing the shining-greatness of God.

And God doesn't only have full peace with Newborns but he loves the Newborns from the bottom of his heart because they belief and appreciate in his son's sacrifice at the cross of Golgotha.

No power can remove, take away or part the eternal godly love to the Newborns, not in heaven and not on earth.

Romans 8, 38-39 (NIV)

For I am convinced that neither death nor life, neither angels nor demons, neither the present nor the future, nor any powers, neither height nor depth, nor anything else in all creation, will be able to separate us from the love of God that is in Christ Jesus our Lord.

It was originally His great, holy, eternal love that the Newborns will not only live and reign in his heavenly kingdom happily and eternally with his son without sorrow, worries and sicknesses but also God has a great, wonderful daily life plan for earthly life **through promises in his word,** dome of those which I as the author accepted and practiced in my religious, work and family life.

For example:

A) Strong and courageous

2.Timothy 1,7 (NLV)

For God did not give us a spirit of fear. He gave us a spirit of power and of love and of a good mind.

Newborn sons and daughters of God can confidently say:

Hebrews 13, 6 (NLV)

So we can say for sure, "The Lord is my Helper. I am not afraid of anything man can do to me."

B) strong self confidence

Philippians 4, 13 (NLV)

I can do all things because Christ gives me the strength.

And Newborns have a string self confidence that their heavenly father made them wonderfully strong and perfectly.

As the psalmist astonished talks to his creator:

Psalm 8, 3 – 8 (NLV)

When I look up and think about Your heavens, the work of Your fingers, the moon and the stars, which You have set in their place, what is man, that You think of him, the son of man that You care for him? You made him a little less than the angels and gave him a crown of greatness and honor. You made him to rule over the works of Your hands. You put all things under his feet: All sheep and cattle, all the wild animals, the birds of the air, and the fish of the sea, and all that pass through the sea.

The psalmist exalts God's works.

C) Bodyguard for the whole life

Our lord Jesus Christ is with the Newborns in their lives really close, much better than a bodyguard with big politicians and very rich people etc. – because Jesus Christ, the son of God, has the same godly power, wisdom, protection as his father, the big creator.

Matthew 28, 20 (NLV)

Teach them to do all the things I have told you. And I am with you always, even to the end of the world.

D) God's navigation system

We have the same spirit that woke Jesus Christ from the dead according to Romans 8, 11 and Galatians 4, 6.

John 16, 13 (NLV)

The Holy Spirit is coming. He will lead you into all truth. He will not speak His Own words. He will speak what He hears. He will tell you of things to come.

The Holy Spirit, who lives in the hearts of the Newborns, not only informs and warns them about spiritual crisis or problems in life, but also gives them God's power, consults them and gives them wisdom on how to solve problems and shows the next steps on the right path.

John 14, 6 (NLV)

Jesus said, "I am the Way and the Truth and the Life. No one can go to the Father except by Me.

Explanation:

Jesus Christ himself is the guidepost through which the GPS system of God (the Holy Spirit) from the worldly apartment address to the new apartment in God's house.

E) Don't give up hope- help in every situation

Hebrews 13, 5 (NLV)

Keep your lives free from the love of money. Be happy with what you have. God has said, "I will never leave you or let you be alone."

God will not leave you alone with unemployment, sudden car breakdown on the highway, scary medical diagnosis, hurricane, tornado etc.

F) Strong counselor-at-law

God does not leave his newborn sons and daughters alone if people try to short-change them with ruthless practices and dubious manipulations.

Romans 8, 31 (NLV)

What can we say about all these things? Since God is for us, who can be against us?

Romans 8, 34 (NLV)

Who then can say we are guilty? It was Christ Jesus Who died. He was raised from the dead. He is on the right side of God praying to Him for us.

G) All serves for our best

Romans 8, 28 (NLV)

We know that God makes all things work together for the good of those who love Him and are chosen to be a part of His plan.

Many followers of Christ, who belong to God's Newborns, are convinced, that everything in their life, even negative and unexpected defeats, serve only their wellbeing and best interest in the end.

H) <u>God's wonderful gifts</u>

The Newborns according to John3, 3 and Galatians 4, 6 have the same spirit as Jesus Christ. They are **always qualified** and ready **(after their New Birth, not before)** for God to **activate** gifts such as speaking tongues, prophecy, healing etc. anytime and in his probability to collect more heavenly fruits and also strengthen their faith in Jesus Christ.

Chapter 10

I.   <u>Relationship</u> of faith of those born again to their Creator

II.   <u>Service</u> of faith for those born again in everyday life

The Newborns are first and foremost **completely convinced** that they can enter the kingdom of heaven through conversion (sin confession/ sin repentance) to live with their heavenly father and his son Jesus Christ as brother eternally, with no end, happily and victorious. And the **newly** Newborns have **two current questions:**

We still live on our blue planet but

<u>First Question:</u>

<u>What does our relationship of faith to our heavenly father every day look like as Newborns?</u>

<u>Second Question:</u>

<u>Service of faith for those born again in everyday life</u>

Answer to the first question:

Relationship of faith of the Newborns to their Creator

1. John 4, 17 (NLV)

Love is made perfect in us when we are not ashamed as we stand before Him on the day He judges.

For we know that our life in this world is His life lived in us.

Romans 5, 2 (NLV)

By putting our trust in God, He has given us His loving-favor and has received us.

We are happy for the hope we have of sharing the shining-greatness of God.

And as guideline for the Newborns for their daily life:

A godly formula for continuous joy and victory:

„The More"

„The more" you are happy in faith, that Jesus Christ, God's son paid and redeemed all punishment for your sins and transgressions, -

„the more" you are God's fragrance and will receive more power, love, joy, health (physically and spiritually) and victory

Answer to the second question:

Service of faith for the Newborns in everyday life

Which everyday services do Newborns have in their new life?

It is God's holy will that the Newborns will not enter the kingdom of heaven **empty handed** (without treasures).

Matthew 6, 20 (NIV)

But store up for yourselves treasures in heaven, where moths and vermin do not destroy, and where thieves do not break in and steal.

Not a single good work of a Newborn will be lost.

Revelation 14, 13 (NLV)

Then I heard a voice from heaven, saying, "Write these words: 'From now on those who are dead who died belonging to the Lord will be happy.'" "Yes," says the Spirit, "they will have rest from all their work. All the good things they have done will follow them."

The especially godly, expensive, eternal, great and valuable treasures, which **Newborns should collect, is the spreading of the Good News** everywhere for anyone – but the **whole Good News**.

It would please our heavenly father as eternal godly treasure that the Newborns (God's sons and daughters) spiritually spread the Good News everywhere in our cities and towns and evoke a big awakening.

It is well known to us that God's word, the bible, consists of many precious and by God inspired books. Here one can use Acts as an example to show that not only the apostles but also the followers of Jesus revolutionized the regions, cities and towns with the Good News.

For example in chapter 11 of Acts the followers of Christ openly declared the Good News in the Arab countries, Sicilia, Macedonia, Greece with unending, passionate, evangelistic efforts.

The number of convinced Christians grew and grew uninterrupted very fast. People converted to the Lord and were baptized. At that time, the people from different social classes left from their houses and huts and came in multitudes to the city centers and gathering places and bazars (grocery stores then) to listen to the good News. And with pure religious joy that their sick were healed they celebrated. This is only an example how at that time the apostles and followers of Jesus (today Newborns) collected fruits with God's power. And before you as a Newborn will take you first step tomorrow in spreading God's word and the Good News, you should know that your creator provides you with the same spiritual tools – as the followers of Christ then.

We have the same son of God

(Because Jesus lives)

Who supports and helps us with our evangelization work. And HE is very happy if we are on our way to spread the Good News about his work of redemption on the cross of Golgotha.

Hebrews 13, 8 (NIV)

Jesus Christ is the same yesterday and today and forever.

We have the same spirit (the Holy Spirit),

as our lord Jesus Christ, God's son, who motivates and directs us as the godly GPS system (Holy Spirit) and protects us from any misery and temptations.

We have God's word even more intense, extensive, and rich

Than then among the first Christian congregations that had only the **Old Testament** and the psalms.

However, we have a wonderful highly developed effective instrument or tool today

Which was not available for the followers of Christ about 2000 years ago as a tool to spread the gospel, the Good News about the work of redemption of Jesus Christ.

And this is the EDV, the Computer, Facebook, Twitter, WhatsApp etc. Through these possibilities, the **newborn**

generation can reach thousands of people in many countries and languages extensively and effectively very easy with the Good News today.

Chapter 11

Short form – comprised in points of the Good News of the New Birth

John 3, 3 (the following verse again)

Jesus replied, "Very truly I tell you, no one can see the kingdom of God unless they are born again."

This **short summary** in points of the Good News of the New Birth, the deliverance and the sacrifice of salvation by Jesus Christ on the cross of Golgotha is very **useful**

a) For the readers of this book as a **quick overview** on the previous pages, the main and core points, how one gets to New Birth and lives it.

b) For convinced Christians and especially pastors, priests, evangelists and so on whose hearts burn to spread the Good News in any daily life task e.g. while on a train or plane to the person sitting next to one and especially on street operations to make the Good News in **points** easily under-

standable and clear to pass on. It is recommended to memorize the following points or even to <u>learn them by heart</u> for God's glory.

Now the comprised short summary about the New Birth in points

Point A

God's word says in the bible in 1 Corinthians 15, 50 that all people on our blue planet don't have a fit body to enter the kingdom of heaven by birth (psalm 51, 7).

Point B

<u>Two terrible</u> reasons exist that make our bodies unfit for the kingdom of heaven

1. Adam's original sin

2. Our own sin

Point C

1. Reason: <u>The original sin</u>

The original sin comes from Adam because he ate from the tree of knowledge against God's will. God was sad and did not only throw him and his wife out of the paradise but this transgression brought <u>damnation upon Adam and Eve</u> and all people.

And through <u>procreation and reproduction</u> their children and children's children were infected by this horrible damned by God virus, the original sin. Today we have about 7 ½ billion people alive and **<u>everyone is infected</u>** with Adam and Eve's original sin.

Romans 5, 18 (and some other verses too)

Consequently, just as one trespass resulted in condemnation for all people, so also one righteous act resulted in justification and life for all people.

Point D

2. Reason: <u>their own sin</u>

The own sins, transgressions and mischiefs that we did years and years and will do again.

<u>Romans 3, 23 –look at chapter 2</u>

Point E

The absolute truth of God is that **only** the people who are <u>free</u> from original and their own sin are allowed to live with God eternally.

Point F

All human and religious efforts and accomplishments, for example through good deeds, healing or gifts as prophecy, speaking in tongues, give charity, donate etc. cannot redeem the original sin or even the smallest own sin (Titus 3, 5).

Point G

No prophets, apostles and all animal burn and sin sacrifices by the priests in the Old Testament, even the popes and leaders of religion could redeem any punishment for sin. God's son, Jesus Christ, is the only one who himself has not sinned in his whole live because he does not originate from Adam and Eve. God, his father, conceived him.

Jesus was conceived

Proof:

1. He was there before Mary was born, even before the universe existed (Ephesians 1, 3-7).

2. The Holy Trinity

3. You gave me a body (in Hebrews)

4. **Genesis 1, 25-26**

Let Us make man like Us.

Jesus was there and helped during his father's act of creation.

Point H

When God saw that his creation was resigned and without hope through all ages, that they had no chance to be redeemed from the original sin and their own sin, it moved his holy heart full of godly love, compassion and mercy and he gave as a **last act** his only dearly loved son as redemptive sacrifice for all sins, misdeeds and transgressions of humanity.

Mark 12, 6

He had one left to send, a son, whom he loved. He sent him last of all, saying, 'They will respect my son.'

John 3, 16-17 (this verse again)

For God so loved the world that he gave his one and only Son, that whoever believes in him shall not perish but have eternal life. For God did not send his Son into the world to condemn the world, but to save the world through him.

Point I

And God watched the exchange, the <u>transaction</u>, that Jesus Christ, the righteous one, who never knew or did sin, carried and redeemed all punishment for every sin, misdeed and transgression of humanity. And God gave his son's righteousness to those who believe in the sacrifice of Jesus Christ.

Point J

If the people who are not born again ask, what they can do to be born new. The answer: do nothing, just believe. And this in 2 steps.

The 1st step, that one believes whole heartedly that Jesus Christ redeemed all sins on Golgotha and one asks God whole heartedly to give the power to be allowed to be born new.

The 2nd step: Confirmation and addition to step 1, that one confesses their sins, as far as one can remember and repents.

Because then the person is a new creation, according to God's word in 2. Corinthians 5, 17. The old body that was infected by the original sin and their own sin was cleaned and redeemed through Jesus Christ's blood on the cross of Golgotha (Romans 6, 6).

The new creation-body is the New Born body and this body is qualified any time and extremely fit to get into the kingdom of heaven eternally and live there happily and victorious. Amen.

Author's final words

The book „Code of eternal life" shows through God's word that every person can enter the kingdom of heaven if one was born new through God's word (the imperishable semen).

1. Peter 1, 23 (NIV)

For you have been born again, not of perishable seed, but of imperishable, through the living and enduring word of God.

One will be born new if the person believes whole-heartedly that

1)

Every human body which origins from Adam and Eve (perishable semen) can absolutely not live with God, the creator in the kingdom of heaven eternally.

2)

Jesus Christ, God's son, redeemed all punishment for every sin thorough Jesus Christ's act of redemption on the cross of Golgotha and additionally confesses their own sin orally and repents. Because then one is born new through God's word with imperishable semen and the body is fit for life in

108

the kingdom of heaven. The big creator confirmed the con-version (sin confession/sin repentance) with great joy through his angels.

Luke 15, 7 (NIV)

I tell you that in the same way there will be more rejoic-ing in heaven over one sinner who repents than over ninety-nine righteous persons who do not need to re-pent.

Luke 15, 10

In the same way, I tell you, there is rejoicing in the pres-ence of the angels of God over one sinner who repents.

Biography of the Author:

Graduate engineer Arsham Kasparian, architect, born 1939 in Basrah, Iraq as son to Armenian parents.

I was raised Armenian-orthodox. I ended my school with the A-levels.

After the A-levels, I did my military service.

Suddenly I had the passionate thought of traveling to Germany.

When I told my family, they laughed at it and said: Why of all things Germany? You do not speak German. Why don't you go to England like your older brother who studied in England? I could not answer that. With approximately converted 600, -- DM in my pockets I began my journey 1966 by train. After 6 days after going through Turkey, Bulgaria, Serbia, Hungary, Austria in Munich/Germany.

As only reference point, I had an address from a neighbor who studied in Friedberg, Germany and I decided to simply go and visit him.

In Munich, I took a cab to ride to Friedberg. In Friedberg near Augsburg, I realized after some searching that my friend did not live in Friedberg/Augsburg but in Friedberg/Hesse. I took another train and soon arrived in Friedberg but my sum of money was already a lot smaller.

To make matters worse my friend was not home. At this time, he was in France. However, the German family with whom my friend lived with was very nice. This strange family offered me to stay with them. It was God's guidance that I met this family.

I came to Germany on a tourist visa but the family took care of me and made sure that I could do an apprenticeship with a building contractor and the authorities extended my residence permit.

My friend returned from his journey; he moved to a different room – I was able to stay with the family. Through the 3 children I learned to speak German fast. With the family's help, I was allowed to take further apprenticeships and another extension of my residence permit. After 2 years, I could start architecture studies in Berlin. This Friedberg-Family were convinced Christians and showed me how I could be Born New through sin confession and repentance, so I experienced a return from my previous life. Through this, I received a personal relationship to God's son and my heavenly father.

My life is impacted up until today to share the Good News with relatives, friends, and everywhere I can – especially in pedestrian zone-campaigns. Trans World Radio transmitted Arabic evangelistic radio shows to me.

For 17 years, I worked for the "Lichtstueble" (marginal group work of evang. Allianz Goeppingen) in Goeppingen voluntary. Since 12 years, I am leading a forum that takes place every first Friday in a month in a Greek restaurant in Salach. More than 120 people from Germany, China, America, Thailand and Malaysia told their testimonies here; that means shared how they met Jesus Christ as personal savior.

On every last Saturday in a month we host a „Breakfast by Kasparian" in our apartment. I get invited to different Christian Congregations to preach there. Usually about the topic "New Birth".

Since 1971, I am married to Edith née Volk from Hessen and our marriage was blessed with three wonderful children as well as sons- and daughters-in-law and especially precious seven grandchildren.

I graduated in 1972 and then worked as an architect in Frankfurt/Main at an international building contractor.

In 1984, we moved to Baden-Wuerttemberg near Goppingen and I was working as a self-employed architect and building contractor until my pension. After my work-life was over – at the age of 65 – I found joy in running and began to run international half-marathons.

In the meantime, – with God's love and help – I succeeded in 17 half-marathons, am joyful, and keep training at the age of almost 79 for new challenges.

Isiah 40, 29 – 31 (NIV)

He gives strength to the weary and increases the power of the weak. Even youths grow tired and weary, and young men stumble and fall; but those who hope in the Lord will renew their strength. They will soar on wings like eagles; they will run and not grow weary, they will walk and not be faint.

As the author, I am willing to evangelize about "Newbirth" anytime and help structure seminars. Contact me under:

Email: arsham.k@web.de

Zeitfracht Medien GmbH
Ferdinand-Jühlke-Straße 7
99095 Erfurt, Deutschland
produktsicherheit@kolibri360.de